The Northern Lights

Susan Canizares

Design: MKR Design, Inc.

Photo Research: Barbara Scott

Endnotes: Susan Russell

JS

—   ˏ

Photographs: Cover: Michio Hoshino/Minden Pictures; p. 1: Gordon Garradd/Science Photo Library/Photo Researchers, Inc.; p. 2: Michio Hoshino/Minden Pictures; p. 3: Jack Finch/Science Photo Library/Photo Researchers, Inc.; p. 4: B & C Alexander/Photo Researchers, Inc.; pp. 5 & 6-7: S. Nielsen/DRK Photo; pp. 8-9: Pekka Parviainen/Science Photo Library/Photo Researchers; pp. 10-11 & 12: S. Neilsen/DRK Photo.

© 1998 by Scholastic Inc.

This edition © 2001 by Scholastic Ltd, Villiers House, Clarendon Avenue, Leamington Spa, Warwickshire CV32 5PR

British Library Cataloguing-in-Publication Data. A catalogue record for this book is available from the British Library.

ISBN 0-439-01939-7

Printed by Lynx Offset Ltd, Chalgrove.

1 2 3 4 5 6 7 8 9 0   1 2 3 4 5 6 7 8 9 0

The night sky is red.

The night sky is yellow.

The night sky is blue.

The night sky is green.

The night sky is purple.

The night sky is

purple and blue.

The night sky is

red and yellow.

The night sky is

purple and green.

What colours do you see?

Northern Lights

On clear nights, far in the north, the skies can be filled with great sheets of shimmering light. The light patterns dance and move and come in many different colours. This amazing display is called the "aurora borealis", or northern lights.

Who gets to see the northern lights? The people who live near the polar regions in countries such as Finland, Canada and Russia can see them. Sometimes, people who live as far south as Scotland get treated to this great light show. The colours of the northern lights are most often frosty white or pale blues and greens, but the lights have been seen in every colour of the rainbow.

What creates the northern lights? Well, the earth is like a huge magnet, and the earth's north and south poles are like the ends of the magnet. The poles attract particles in the atmosphere that are tiny bits of energy. Some of these bits of energy come from the sun and they are called solar particles. Sometimes, the sun puts out extra amounts of energy and creates what we call solar flares. This greater amount of solar energy gives rise to the northern lights.

These extra solar particles flow around and around the earth, but in outer space. As they flow, they sometimes come near the north and south poles of the earth. And because the poles are the ends of the earth's magnet, they capture some of the solar particles, bringing them into the earth's atmosphere. Now the particles collide with gaseous particles already in the atmosphere. When they collide like this, they give off light and the light is what we see in the sky. This spectacular effect is called the aurora. Shown in this book is the "aurora borealis" in the far north. In the far south, this light show is called the "aurora australis".